GW00633031

Experiences in Life
A Selection of Poems

Gillian McCahey

ARTHUR H. STOCKWELL LTD.
Torrs Park Ilfracombe Devon
Established 1898
www.ahstockwell.co.uk

British Library Cataloguing-in-Publication Data.
A catalogue record for this book is available
from the British Library.

ISBN 978-0-7223-3788-2
Printed in Great Britain by
Arthur H. Stockwell Ltd.
Torrs Park   Ilfracombe
Devon

CONTENTS

THE VICTORY

The flat is sold, the battle won,
Now I can relax and have some fun.
I have so many boxes there will not be room
As the day of moving begins to loom.

My friend Adele has been by my side,
With many things I did confide.
Tomorrow we hope to celebrate;
So much we can both relate.
We will have a meal beside the sea
To talk about my 'victory'.

I have a flag that I will fly
As to my home I will say Goodbye.
Goodbye to all that is left behind,
A better future I will hope to find.

I will have a home at Rosey Bay –
Will be the best in every way.
Amidst the rabbits, birds and trees
I can go for walks and breathe with ease.

I can do my art, enjoy the sun,
I might even swim, walk or run!
My weight endeavour to reduce,
Until my clothes become baggy and loose.
A different figure I will hope to be
Because of my final 'victory'.

MOVING DAY

At last I am here at the above address
After many a week in such a mess.
The day to move I did not know,
My mind worked so hard I was feeling low.

At last I got the date to move,
The things to clear and to improve.
I had so much rubbish you would never know,
It worried me things piled up so much so.

Then my friends they came to my aid,
The things in cupboards so neatly laid.
The china, books, the boxes unpacked;
By the time it was finished we all were whacked.

My home and belongings began to shape,
The rubbish all cleared after using a rake,
The garbage bags all filled to the brim –
Prior to this things were looking grim.

As soon as all was looking neat
I sat in the chair and rested my feet.
Out of the window a view I see
And everything is looking so lovely.

Maggie, my cat, she looked around –
No rubbish now could be found.
Now she's clear of that awful mess.
The next move I hope will be less and less.
Boxes here, boxes there –
Where we were going I did not know where.

Can I settle and sit on her knee?
I believe her move went successfully.
Though in a few days' time we had to go
Whether it was windy, rain or snow.

I can look ahead with God's help each day,
For I know He will help me in every way.
I also have plenty of good friends around,
Although things looked as a great big mound.

Gradually the mound now has ceased
And now my pleasures have increased,
I can do my art and crosswords too,
Go for a walk, a drive or two.

The spring and summer will soon appear –
I do enjoy that time of year.
My decking with pots of bulbs and flowers –
Then will come the April showers.

Look to the future I will hope to see
All worked out successfully.
At times the clouds were looking black;
Now I own a home without a lack.

A view from the window out to the sea –
All worked out so well for me.
My fears and troubles now have passed
And I can relax and rest at last.

THE PLUMBER

My advice I give to you –
The experiences I had were but a few:
Don't ever have a plumber without a choice.
I will tell you this with all my voice.

I moved into a lovely home
To find the carpets soaking wet.
The plumber I had was with regret.
The work that was done was a disgrace –
I do not know how he could show his face.

Inferior work that he had done –
I did not think was any fun.
The materials used were very poor –
I am sure it was against the law.

I paid a lot for this new home,
Am sure I am not alone.
Others here have had the same
Who could at an individual point the blame.

They would say it was not me!
I was away in Alderney.
The carpets now are drying out –
I am saying this with so much doubt.

Will this last a few more days?
This I will be very amazed.
Will more water be found?
This I will have to look around.

If I find another fault
I will not take it with a pinch of salt.
To a solicitor I will go;
To him I will take my fears and woe.

I will tell him this and that
And with compensation I will get fat.
Why should I put up with all?
The plumber, his renown will take a fall.

He will be called to task for the work he did
And many a customer he will lose.
Him again they will not choose.
This a warning you will take –
Do not again make this mistake.

A WINDY DAY

The wind blew and blew, the house did shake,
The noise was such I am kept awake.
The washing lines with fluttering clothes –
Vests, pants and shirts – whose are those?

The washing lines with half washing left –
Was it the wind? or was it theft?
Where are my socks? Where are my blouses?
Half were blown over the tops of the houses.

The wind blew and blew, the sun was gone.
When was the last time it had shone?
Behind the clouds it peeped its head
In and out; the sun then it fled.

CONVERSATION BETWEEN THE SUN AND WIND

Sun: "Shall I shine or sleep today?
The people are coming out on holiday.
The raindrops fall practically every day,
Why should I shine for them today?"

The wind he said, "I will blow today.
I do not care if they are on holiday.
The children in the sand can play,
I will blow and blow without delay."

The sun at last poked out his head:
"I am going to shine till they are red.
I am tired of sleeping each and every day,
I will come out and watch them play."

Wind: "I hear the laughter and the fun."
The sun is out, the wind did shun.
"I am going to calm myself today;
Instead I will go to bed, I have had my day.
I will watch the sunshine from my bed,
I will go to rest and sleep instead."

All is calm, the sun is out,
I do not know what *you* shout about.

MY LITTLE ROVER METRO

My Rover Metro has been a bane –
Took to the garage again and again,
Had it serviced and MOT'd,
Money was taken by the garage with some speed.

My Rover Metro has been my friend.
Before this happened I could depend.
At Rosey Bay I am out in the sticks –
I am in a state and in a fix.

Took it to the garage as *again* broke down,
The garage man looked at it and gave a frown.
To the diagnostic machine it must go,
To find what fault I do not know.

A new sensor is required, they did say.
I looked at the mechanic with dismay.
Drove it home, hoped it would last,
Thought the problem was solved and past.

Attempted next morning to start the car –
Stopped again, and I did not get far.
"What shall I do this time?" I said.
This thought again went through my head.

I know what I will do, I will call the AA,
As I have tried to start my car *another* day.
The AA man came and looked at my car:
"With this engine you will not go far!"

"I will contact the breakdown people," he said.
"I am afraid your car is surely dead."
He spent some time and tried so hard.
It will have to go to the breakers' yard.

To my poor car I said Goodbye –
In the past I could rely.
"You have taken me here and taken me there;
You may think that I do not care.

"Your engine is now beyond repair,
As I look on you with *more* despair.
You have been a friend for many years –
I say Goodbye with many tears."

THE PETTY FIGHT

There were two girls on the Isle of Wight
Who started off a petty fight.
"That thing's *mine*! and not yours at all.
I bought that nice big ball.
My pocket money *I* used to buy.
How is it *yours*? You tell me why!

"Anyway, I am the eldest of us two,
So there! I will play with my best friend, Sue.
She is not the same age as you or me,
She will not argue, *she* will agree.

"I would rather make friends with her than you,
It does not matter between us two.
We will keep the peace and, all tension to release,
Come! we will all play together.
The sun is shining and lovely weather.

"There is no excuse for us to fight,
Which we have been doing from morn till night.
Let us be friends and stop this quarrelling –
Maybe we could share or do some borrowing.

"You have the ball one day and me the next,
It will stop us continually getting vexed.
Life is too short to keep a fight –
To see friends playing is a lovely sight!

"I am now glad we can play, skip and run
And really have some lovely fun.
We can all play together,
And enjoy the sun and lovely weather.
Stop the fight and let us be friends" –
And that is the story how it ends.

THE SELLING OF A FRIEND'S HOUSE

Poor Adele has been through hell.
Her house on the market would not sell:
She tried so hard to keep it nice,
And asked the agent for advice.

"What shall I do?" she said to him.
"The sale of my house is looking grim."
He said, "Pack your things into a box."
She said, "I have worked off my cotton socks.

"Days and days have passed me by
Until I began to sigh and sigh.
What shall I do? I have worked in vain,
I have tried again, again and again.

"There have been some the house to see
But I still have not gained the victory.
My hopes were up, my hopes were down,
Now I am beginning to fret and frown.

"Why is it going on so long?
I am wondering what house I will soon belong.
I have looked at this, and I looked at that.
Will I have a house? Will I have a flat?
Some are big, some are small,
It is impossible to view them all."

At last she decided to make a move,
Leave the house empty, and things to improve.
"It is not easy," she began to say,
"But I will move without further delay.

"I cannot possibly bear any more.
So I decided to temporarily move to Bodmin Moor.
Spot and me will go together,
Because now I have reached the end of my tether.

"Bowswater I will not be sorry to leave;
Hope my worries and troubles to relieve.
I still have to go to the faraway shop
And work and work till I am ready to flop.

"I had hoped to retire and rest my head.
I am so tired I will take to my bed.
My head and my brain keep whirling around,
Hoping some answer will soon be found.

"How long will I work to pay my bills?
To work so hard and have no thrills?
Day after day I live in hope,
Wondering how much longer I will cope.
I say to myself a light will shine
And all will soon be looking fine."

THE NOMAD
(A True Nonsense Poem)

It all began in the year 2003,
All because my roof leaked, you see.
The parapet and the ceilings were taken down,
Which made me fret and made me frown.

All my belongings, the cat and me
Were moved three times – January, November, February –
The years 2003 and 2004.
I felt I could not stand any more.

The car was vandalised and taken to be repaired;
Now I am getting more and more grey-haired.
I have a good friend named Adele;
I am glad she helped me to cope so well.

We texted each other to have a chat,
We talked over this and over that.
We went for walks to share our load,
She picked me up along the road.
I packed my belongings and loaded her car,
She helped me unload and said Ta-ta!

Kindly she phoned me to check I was all right,
Wished me well and said Goodnight.
My cat woke me up and nipped my ear –
She stays by my side and stays very near.

Today I awoke to a layer of snow,
Which is very white and a lovely glow.
The beautiful sight is good to see;
I am glad I have the cat for company.

GOD'S CREATION

The wonder of Nature is good to see,
All things created so wonderfully –
God's handiwork in the trees and the flowers,
The sun shining through the April showers.

The butterflies painted with beautiful colours,
Birds building nests with many others,
The lambs skipping in the fields,
The farmers sowing to get some yields.

God's handiwork we cannot deny
When we see the rainbows in the sky,
Breezes, sunbeams, leaves unfold –
So many beauties we can behold.

Look to Nature and what it brings:
New life and so many wonderful things.
All these things bring cheer when we are low –
Beauty above, the same below.

THE FARMER'S LAMENT

I worked so hard throughout the year,
Ploughed and sowed and shed a tear.
The storms and wind blew very hard,
I drove the cattle through the yard.

There is muck and mud, the cattle low,
Was it worth my labour the seed to sow?
The wheat was ripe and good to see,
But now wind and rain came regretfully.

The barns were ready to be filled,
The corn and flour to be milled;
But now an empty barn I see
When I have toiled from morn till tea.

I look with hope, next year will be
All the harvest gathered successfully.
I say to myself, 'Do not look back –
Next year there won't be lack.'

Every year is different – there will be a crop
Even though I work till I do flop.
Each experience brings a lesson that is taught.
The battle will be won that I have fought.

God always works in mysterious ways.
He sees the future of my days,
He hides each step from my view,
He lifts all burdens for me and you.

A FRIEND IN TIME OF NEED
(An Experience in a Holiday Park)

There is a friend at Rosey Bay.
He is so good in every way.
He gives a hand where there is need,
Although 'owners' take cash with speed.

To this friend we go to tell our woes.
The days we have are highs and lows.
One day we are up, then days we are down.
This friend we have deserves a crown.

In weeks to come we have to go
To face the winter and the snow.
A place to live we have to find –
We have no home of any kind.

We sold our homes to live out here;
We cannot stay throughout the year.
We have no landline to phone our friends,
No vote, no post, we follow trends.

We have now a mobile phone to use,
Not at all that we would choose.
At the General Store we buy our goods:
Our daily paper and our foods.

Instead we have to go to town
As now our shop is closing down.
End of this month this will take place;
We have to accept it all with grace.

Now to lodgings we must go,
A room or flat we do not know.
Will it be warm? Will it be cold?
We had to do what we were told.

In March we hope to here return.
We will be wise and all discern.
We hope improvements we will find
And less restrictions of any kind.

Our plant pots, boxes, and our sheds,
Our verandas, flowers, blues and reds –
We will make our homes as good as can be.
Will we all gain a victory?

FINDING A DENTIST

To find a dentist on the National Health,
You will instead go private and must have wealth.
We have searched here and searched there,
And cannot find one anywhere.

And now our teeth are going bad,
We really think it's very sad.
When was the last time we had some fillings?
As years ago it cost only shillings.

Today we must now have to wait.
When our teeth decay it is too late.
The dentist has to pull them out,
Which makes us cry and makes us shout.

The dentist said, "Why did you wait?
Your teeth are in an awful state."
We said to him, "We have looked here and looked there,
To find a dentist was very rare."

Our teeth are bad and now decayed,
And now our bills we have paid and paid.
Our cash is almost now diminished,
When now our treatment at last has finished.

The dentist said, "You will need false teeth."
We looked aghast with unbelief.
It is not *our* fault, we let him know:
"Natural teeth we would rather show."

Gleaming false teeth there now will be,
And now a smile our friends will see.
No gaps or fillings will be found,
No dentist will we look around.

At last our worries now have ceased,
Now that our teeth have now decreased.
The dentist rubbed both hands with glee –
The new dentures he now can see.

"Are you glad you came to me
And brought bad teeth for me to see?
I know you wished you came before;
The state of them was very poor.

"I hope your friends will come to me,
But they will have to pay a fee.
It is best they come at an earlier stage
Before their teeth go bad with age."

MOGGY

My name is Moggy, I have my way
And like the food my choice every day.
Am rather finicky and very fussy,
But still I am a lovely pussy.

I follow my owner wherever she goes;
If I am not on her lap, I lie at her toes.
In the bathroom, kitchen and lounge,
Wonder what food I can scrounge?

I am loved and petted – what more could I want? –
And wake up my owner at six o'clock prompt,
To nudge her or nip her ear,
For I make a loud purr to make her hear.

Each time her case is packed to go away,
I look at her with some dismay.
Why are you leaving me to see your friends?
On food and comfort my life depends.

Miss her so much when she goes away:
As I look out of the window day after day.
The hours and minutes go round the clock,
Tick-tock, tick-tock, tick-tock.

The days go by and the time draws near,
And to the door I give my ear.
Is she coming or is she not?
She went away and me forgot.

For to hear the handle turned at the door,
And hope she stays – it is half past four!
Time for my meal and a sit on her lap,
A drink of milk when she takes off the cap.

Only the best is all I desire.
After my meal I will sit by the fire.
Will *not* have a mat, it *must* be a rug.
Off to sleep and I am nice and snug.

BUSY WORLD

The world is so busy,
People get all in a tizzy
Rushing to and fro, up and down,
A lot are wearing a permanent frown.

If only they would pause and take their time.
To be less harrassed, all would be fine!
Work has to be done and chores to do,
So much for them, me, and you.

Many look forward to take their ease,
To go on holiday and do as they please.
Not so easy as it may seem,
To take a break and fulfil a dream.

Today people work over the retirement age
As they now earn only the minimum wage.
By the time they are ready to rest their heads,
Unfortunately they have to take to their beds!

Children grow up and work so hard,
To their parents they have so little regard.
Struggling to raise money to buy a house,
So much to make them grumble and grouse.

They must look forward with every hope,
Things will change to help them cope.
It *will* get better as time goes by.
There will be those they can rely.

OUR WINDOW

We can look to the horizon to see the ships pass
And imagine the lucky ones travelling first class.
Can they see us on the land from there?
Where are they going? We would like to know where?

We are waiting for the sunshine, instead of rain.
No, it is raining again and again.
The wind blows hard day after day
And we wish we could go on our holiday.

The time has come when we will have some fun.
We can lie on the beach and enjoy the sun.
Children will build sandcastles in the sand.
Everything will look and feel so grand.

It was worth waiting for fine weather to see.
Wonderful to sit beside the sea.
Everything working out well for you and I.
Tomorrow we hope will be sunny and dry.

We will relax and take our ease.
Go for a walk and do as we please.
Have an ice cream or go for a swim.
In a few days we will be getting slim.